WHATT FETTLE, MUN!

A CELEBRATION OF CUMBRIAN DIALECT

TIM BARKER

WITH ILLUSTRATIONS BY
RICHARD SCOLLINS

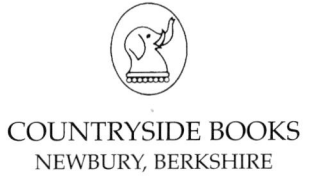

COUNTRYSIDE BOOKS
NEWBURY, BERKSHIRE

First published 2007
© Tim Barker, 2007

COUNTRYSIDE BOOKS
3 Catherine Road
Newbury, Berkshire

To view our complete range of books,
please visit us at
www.countrysidebooks.co.uk

ISBN 978 1 84674 053 4

Both publisher and author acknowledge with gratitude the debt they owe to *Ey Up Mi Duck!* by Richard Scollins and John Titford, first published in 1976. That book was the inspiration for the series of regional dialect volumes of which this is one.

Designed by Peter Davies, Nautilus Design
Produced through MRM Associates Ltd., Reading
Typeset by CJWT Solutions, St Helens
Printed by Cambridge University Press

*All material for the manufacture of this book
was sourced from sustainable forests.*

CONTENTS

INTRODUCTION

The Lake District and Cumbria

Yer b'yuk-larn'd wise gentry, what's seen many coonties
May preach an' palaver an' brag as they will
O' moontans, lakes, valleys, woods, watters an' medders
But canny auld Cummerlan caps 'em aw' still.

Robert Anderson

In 1965 Carlisle United won promotion to Division Two of the Football League — what would now be the Championship — and TV commentator Frank Bough looked forward to seeing a lowly team from the wilds of northwestern England playing the legendary Wolverhampton Wanderers, who had just been relegated. As it turned out Carlisle's first home game of the new season was not against the Wolves, but the sheep were out in force. BBC cameras were at Brunton Park, and the director was at great pains to focus on the flocks grazing by the river Eden, just outside the ground. Since then United fans (who have produced some of the worst soccer thugs in the country, but are generally a good-humoured and imaginative bunch) have revelled in being branded thorough country hicks. The team mascot is a fox, but what Cumbrians brandished at Wembley when The Blues won the Auto Windscreens Shield in 1997 were inflatable sheep. We're proud of our sheep; we're proud of our farming heritage; and we're proud of our local twang, which has cheered county teams to victory at Lords and Twickenham as well as the now defunct Twin Towers.

Strictly speaking Carlisle itself lies outside the Lake District, and the citizens speak with an accent influenced by Geordie, with a touch of Scots. They don't sound like the people of the Lakes at all. That's the trouble with dialects; they differ from town to town, never mind region to region. Until 1974 the Lake District lay within three counties: Cumberland, Westmorland, and the Furness district of Lancashire. These were then amalgamated and called Cumbria, a historic name denoting the distinct political and geographic region stretching from the river Esk on the Scottish border down to Morecambe Bay. A look at the map shows it surrounded by sea on three sides: the Solway Firth to the North, the Irish Sea to the West and Morecambe Bay to the South. The eastern boundary is the Pennines. Cumbria was once a kingdom in its own right, and for a time it belonged to Scotland. During this period the title Prince of Cumberland was the Scottish equivalent of Prince of Wales. The plot of Shakespeare's *Macbeth* hinges on this fact, so that when the king's son Malcolm is made Prince of Cumberland Macbeth realizes he'll have to move fast if he wants to be king himself and he embarks on the killing spree that finally brings him down.

Round the rim of the present county lie the English Border lands and Carlisle, the western edge of the Pennines, the industrial belt of West Cumbria, and the Furness area round Barrow, but at the centre and dominating the region are the mountains and waters of the Lake District — the bit people have heard of, the bit in the tourist guides, the bit like no other in the world. The language here is also like no other, and is as sturdy and rugged as the mountains. This book makes no claim to be a serious study of it, but it does take a look at the lighter side of the language and the people and way of life that shaped it. *We'll nut ev thuh laffin at us, but thoo's welcome to laff wid us!*

5

CHAPTER 1

Whee started it? The dialect(s) of Cumbria and the Lake District

Blame it on the Vikings; it's usually a safe plan.

The dialect of the Lakes is an ancient way of talking and naturally contains elements of all the languages that invading *oot'ners* and *off-cummers* have brought to this most remote and most remarkable corner of England. You can tell from the place-names. For example, south of Carlisle and on the very edge of the Lakeland *Fells* (from an Old Norse word for 'hill') lies *Torpenhow*, named after the hill, such as it is, where the village stands. To one tribe of ancient Britons, who spoke a form of Celtic close to Cornish and Breton, the word for a hill was *Tor* (e.g. Glastonbury Tor), so when they'd climbed to the top they called it the Tor. Up the Tor some time later marched other Ancient Britons. They asked the natives, 'What d'you call this place?' and the natives, looking round at the land going downwards in every direction, said 'We call it the *Tor* – what else would you call it?'

Now these other Ancient Britons spoke a form of Celtic close to Welsh and their name for a hill was *Pen*, just like in Welsh (e.g. Penmaenmawr, Penyghent) so the little settlement became Tor Pen.

Centuries later, to the place now called Hill Hill came the Vikings. They weren't the hairy burners, pillagers and rapists of legend but a later generation who arrived from Ireland and the Isle of Man where the burners, pillagers, etc. had settled down and become respectable. In their turn they asked, 'What d'you call this place?' and the natives told them, and, in their turn, they called it Torpen Hill. And as you've guessed, the Viking word for hill was *How*[1] and to this day you can visit Hill Hill Hill off the A595 between Carlisle and Cockermouth.

Various Celtic words lingered on and are more common here than in many other English counties. As in Wales, the dark little Britons clung on in the mountains, and the name *Cumbria* has the same root as the Welsh word for Wales, *Cymry*. Basically, it just means 'folk'.

---

[1] Old Norse *How* is related to Old English *heah* which means 'high' – but don't ask me how.

Hints of Celtic appear in the famous shepherds' count. When counting sheep (at work, not in bed), Lakeland shepherds traditionally worked in twenties using a system of numbers peculiar to themselves and more than peculiar to everyone else. Most of the words are probably just made-up nonsense – like *eeny meeny miney mo* – but they do have some affinities with Welsh. The Lakeland Dialect Society's journal for 1994 lists six Cumbrian versions of the list plus three from Yorkshire and one from Ayrshire[2]. Details varied from valley to valley, but most systems begin *yan, tan, tethera*, which is well enough known to have been used as the title of an opera by Harrison Birtwistle, based on a poem by Tony Harrison. Neither of them is Cumbrian but they both set great store by being professional Northerners.

The counting system I know goes:

1 yan	6 sethera	11 yan a dick	16 yan a bumfit
2 t'yan	7 lethera	12 t'yan a dick	17 t'yan a bumfit
3 tethera	8 hovera	13 tethera dick	18 tethera bumfit
4 methera	9 dovera	14 methera dick	19 methera bumfit
5 pimp	10 dick	15 bumfit	20 jigget

Some of these are similar to Welsh: *un* (1), *pymp* (5), *dec* (10), but Welsh numbers are nicked from Latin anyway. As for *jigget* (20); spell it *gigot* and every

Is thoo aw reet number 16?

Come in number 91; Thi time's up

We hevven't got a 91

9035. The Boat Station and Catbells. Derwentwater, Keswick.

---

[2] The article also points out that no one after about 1800 admits to actually hearing any shepherds use such numbers!

7

twentieth sheep was clearly marked down for eating. *Yan* continues very definitely to be the Lakeland word for 'one'.

On the other hand several dialect words for sheep themselves are from Old Norse. *Yow* means 'ewe'; a *gimmer* is a yearling sheep, a *twinter* a two-year-old and a *hog* is last year's lamb. It's definitely the Norse element which helps to make Lakeland language distinctive: every place-name containing *thwaite* (clearing) or *holm* (island), and every word beginning with *sk-* is a relic of the Vikings, as are the very *becks* and *tarns*. The Norse influence on Lakeland dialect goes beyond mere vocabulary. Apparently the least changed of all the ancient Scandinavian languages is Icelandic and it's uncannily similar to Cumbrian. William Rollinson, whose *Cumbrian Dictionary of Dialect, Tradition and Folklore* is a must if you want to learn more, says 'with conviction' from personal experience that our dialect is understood in Iceland. Melvyn Bragg (see p. 34), recalls eating in a restaurant in Scandinavia and hearing what to him was pure Cumbrian dialect as a native on his way out said, As *garn yam* 'I'm going home'.

By the way, if anyone who paid attention during their history lessons is asking 'Where did the Anglo-Saxons come in?', just remember that Lakeland is a dialect of English, and that the Angles and Saxons provided many of the other words that are common to English speakers everywhere[3].

As well as exotic vocabulary, Lakelanders sometimes employ an exotic grammar. It can't be denied (Who wants to deny it? We're proud of it.) that, cut off in our mountain lairs, we could be slow to adapt and certainly fell a bit behind the rest of the country in speech patterns. Lakeland dialect retains much of the grammar of Shakespeare and the King James Bible with *thee* and *thou* occurring frequently along with their accompanying verb forms: *Dost thou?*, *Hast thou?*, *Wilt thou?*, etc. Listen carefully, though, because the pronunciations can be slippery. Those mentioned actually come out as *Duster?*, *Hester?* and *Wilter?*. And we get a bit confused with our verb forms: not *I am* and *thou art* but *I is* and *thou is* (pronounced *ah's* and *thoo's*); so that *What art thou doing* becomes *What ist thou doing?* (and sounds like *Whatt's tuh d'yern?*).

Which brings us to the matter of accent and the major problem with books about dialect – how do you write it down? Much that distinguishes one dialect from another is not a question of vocabulary or grammar but simply of pronunciation, and lots of so-called dialect words are just everyday English ones pronounced with a regional accent. Lakeland speakers don't think of them as any different from the ones that other people like the Queen or BBC announcers or

---

[3] If anyone really paid attention during history lessons and wants to know about any Norman influence, well Cumbria doesn't feature in Domesday Book because the Normans never got into the mountains properly.

Australians use. They just think the word *grass* sounds better when it rhymes with gas[4] than when it rhymes with farce.

The long *o* sound is a prime example. At the end of words such as barrow or fellow, it degrades to a general grunt like the *-er* on the end of father or letter. In the middle of words such as road or lone, it's pronounced as in paw. If we were to play the game of writing dialect phrases as if they were uttered in RP (received pronunciation), we could have *saw a sword a gnawed caught* for what Lakelanders would make of 'so I sewed an old coat'. To ask a driver if he was familiar with the official manual of road safety one would say *Duster nought he weigh cord*? So a Windermere *boat* sounds like RP 'bought', but 'I'm aboard a boat I bought about a week ago' becomes *As aboard abort about a boot a week sin*.

The *Concise Oxford* confirms the great problem with written English: you can't write a combination of letters and know that they'll always sound the same. Linguists with their phonetic alphabet might be able to transcribe the errant sounds but the rest of us have no such skill. Those who've written in dialect over the years – especially posh speakers putting it on – usually try to suggest how the words actually sound, but they generally assume their readers know what they should be hearing anyway. No two writers seem to spell the stuff the same way, and some words almost defy transcription. The Lakeland pronunciation of 'do' for instance has been written *deu* or *diu*, and my own inclination is to spell it *dyer*, except that you would probably rhyme that with dire. The word is just completely different from any other. For a start the vowel sound is nothing to do with either the letter *o* or the letter *u*; it's the same as the one in her. Fair enough, but after the *d* and before the vowel comes an intrusive *y* sound, similar to Geordie, so the thing starts like the word 'duty'. It's practically identical to the French word for god, *dieu*, and from hereon it's going to be spelt *d'yer*. So *d'yer thi best ter remimber*!

The intrusive *y* crops up continually in the dialect (see *f'yass*, *l'yam*, etc) and is sometimes inserted into most unlikely places. Silloth's amateur dramatic society was once rehearsing a play in which a well-to-do couple discuss their holiday in Italy: 'It happened in Rome, my dear.' 'N'yaples, Tom.'

A long *e* often replaces a short one before *d* (*reed* for 'red', *heed* for 'head', *deed* for 'dead') but can also replace *i* (*hee* for 'high', *leet* for 'light') or even *o* in the word 'so': *Ah got see clarty, ah hed to hev a wesh* ("I got so messy, I had to have a wash"). You'll notice from that example that the displaced short *e* gets revenge by taking over the *a* sounds in *hev a wesh*. It also replaces long *a* in *med*

---

[4] Gas of course is not intended to rhyme with guess; Upper Class Britons speak a dialect of their own.

A Local L'yerk at Nursery Rhymes

Little Jack Horner

'made' and perhaps dispossesses *u* in *sec* 'such', though the difference there is so great that *sec* deserves to be taken as a genuine dialect word rather than a variant pronunciation.

Cumbrians generally pronounce their aitches – *'e* for 'he' and *'is* for 'his' are exceptions – but often drop their ells, as in *kick't baw ower't waw an' it'll faw into't haw* 'Kick the ball over the wall and it will fall into the hall'. If it rolls 'through the door onto the floor of the tower', however, that's *through't dooer onto't flooer o't tooer*, while 'four strangers on a tour' would be *fower offcummers on a tower*.

In the middle of words *th* often turns into *d*: *Ah seed Fadder wid Mudder. She wes bledderin' on as usual.*

Finally a word about the typical Northern equivalent of 'the'. If pronounced at all, it's simply *t* and in the middle of a phrase it's best to think of it as coming after the previous word rather than before the next one: *She went into t' hoose to gan to t' toilet.* If it's the first word in a phrase, it's sounded before a vowel and creeps in before consonants when it can (e.g. *t' laal un's bawlin agyan*) but is often so tentative that it's hardly pronounced at all, certainly not before a word beginning with *t* or *d*. Definitely avoid the temptation to put it in twice before vowels (*we're goin' fer a drink in t t'inn*, for example), as this is only done by Southerners sending up the dialect and by Yorkshire people who don't understand their own grammar.

CHAPTER 2

Dickshinry

a'	on: *Thoo wassn't i' church a' Sunda.*
aa	I. (It can be long like *ah* or short like *a* depending on context.)
ab'yern	above
afoor	before
ahint	behind
allus	always
anenst	next to
ask	a lizard (**dry ask**) or newt (**watter ask**)
aw	all
ax	to ask. (*Aa axed me mam an' dad* does not mean the speaker is Lizzie Borden.)
back word	*to give back word*: to pull out of a deal, such as buying a house
bairn or **barn**	a child
blait	nervous: *a blait cat meks a bowld moose*
blaw	to blow. (At wrestling bouts an entrant's name is called three times. If he doesn't enter the ring he's *blawn oot* and forfeits the contest.)
bledder	to blather; babble
blittered	storm-damaged (for example, a building)
boggart or **boggle**	a goblin or scary spirit

In a dialect poem on Shakespeare's *A Midsummer Night's Dream*, the king of the fairies

> *Calls till is aid a canny laal boggart ca'd Puck,*
> *An tells im to flee till the back o' beyont,*
> *A magical flooer to pluck.*

braffen	a horse collar (see GURNIN' THROUGH A BRAFFEN p. 51). Also **braffum**
	(My own guess is that braffen is a version of *brougham* and that the collar is associated with the carriage of the same name. But see BROUGHAM in *Local Place Names* p. 29.)
brant	steep
brat	an apron
bray	verb = to hit, strike, beat; noun = a hit, blow: *If't ingine won't start, give it a bray.*
	(F.J. Carruthers in *Lore of the Lake Country* says there are no fewer than 109 dialect words meaning to beat or strike.)
broo	a hill
brummle	a blackberry
brussen	broken
butter shag	a knob of butter dipped in sugar and given as a treat: *Bad bairns gits nee butter shags.*
b'yerk	a book
by gow!	a Lakeland exclamation, equivalent of *by gum!* or *by heck!* Also **by the cringe! lawvin days!**
byre	a cowshed. (In the south of the county they sometimes say *shuppon* or *shippon* but that's really a Lancashire word. Conversely those who use shippon would claim that *byre* is a Scottish word. Both are from Old English.)
cap	to beat or perhaps crown: *That caps cock-fightin!* That is amazing!
capped	pleased: *'E wuz fair capped.* He was pleased as Punch.
cannel	a candle
canny	good; careful, sharp. (*A gey canny businessman might live a canny way off* and if the roads were bad you might have to *ga canny.*)
clart or clarty	mess or messy. With a general suggestion of stickiness – mud, jam and old mashed potato are *clarty.*
clart aboot	to fool around: *Sk'yerl winder's brok. T' laal uns wuz clartin aboot.*

The Old Bridge House, Ambleside.

'Bijou detached residence. All-round views. Running water.'

A Local L'yerk at Nursery Rhymes

Humpty Dumpty

cloot or **clout** 1. cloth or an item of clothing: *Ne'er cast a cloot till may is oot;* 2. a blow: *Aa'll gi' thuh sec a cloot if thoo doesn't shut thi gob.*

coo a cow; **coo clap** cow pat

cop to catch: *Cop hod o't' r'yap* Get hold of the rope.

cower or **cowie** a thing, a whatsit. See also SCRAN

cowp to fall

crack noun = talk, convivial chat: *Ther wuz grand crack in't pub toneel.* verb = to talk, chatter: *Jonty wuz crackin' on aboot is granfadder in't' fust worrald wahr.* (It may be related to Irish craic.)

cuddy a donkey. (A schoolboy with prominent ears might be nicknamed *Cuddylugs.*)

cuddy wifted left-handed

cush! an exclamation used to add emphasis: *Cush, mun, Aa nivver seed oot like it.*

cushat a wood pigeon

c'yak cake: *buthda c'yak wid cannels on't; Kersmas c'yak*

dab *Nivver lit dab* Don't tell anyone.

daft man to make a fool of; bamboozle:

'Hoo dusta git folk to buy thi double glazin?'

'Aa daft man em.'

dee/deed die/dead

deef deaf

deek to look (at). (This is a linguist's dream. It's an adaptation of Hindi *dekho* 'look!', which came to Britain with old sweats from the Indian army. They would say 'Let's have a dekko', which in Cumbria became 'Let's have a deek' but was fully adopted into dialect in phrases like *Deeks tuh yon* Look at that.)

dinner lunch; see also SUPPER

divvent don't

dook a swim; to swim: *Aa warnt say he's fat; but when he gans dookin' at Ravenglass, tide cums in at Maryport.*

dookers bathing drawers

doot	doubt. However, *aa doot* = I'm sure: *'E's nivver gawin ter marry her?' 'Aa doot e is.'*
dowly	glum: *Thoo's as dowly as a wet weekend.*
dusta	do you? (dost thou?)
d'yer	to do:
	Customer: *Dusta d'yer real ale?*
	Barman: *Nee, Aa divvent.*
	Customer: *Dusta d'yer keg?*
	Barman: *Aye, Aa d'yer.*
	Customer: *Then aa'll ev a whiskey.*
dyke	earth embankment; wall; hedge
efter	after
fair	thoroughly: *Aa wuz fair clemmed* I was starving.
famous	very good: *E's a famous wrussler.*
fash	to fret; to worry
feckless	idle and incompetent; useless

Bus Stop Scene 1

Divvent fash. E'll nut hurt Thuh.

Git him off muh!

fell	a mountain. The Fells include
	Scafell (*Skawfell*) Pike (at 3,218 ft it's England's highest mountain)
	Skiddaw (*Skidder*), second highest (3,053 ft)
	Saddleback (Blencathra)
	Cat Bells; Catstycam (*Cat stick em*)
	Dollywagon Pike
	Seat Sandal
	Robinson – no relation of ...
	The Old Man of Coniston – or indeed of
	Pike o' Blisco – or ...
	Stybarrow Dod
fettle	verb = to fix. Like *fix*, it can mean either repair or almost the exact opposite: *Aa skelpt is lug. That fettled im;* noun = state of health: *Noo then marra. Whatt fettle?* Good Day old friend. How are you?; *'E won't can gan tilt pub. 'E's o' bad fettle.* He'll be unable to visit the hostelry. He's rather poorly.
	After Roger Bannister ran the first four-minute mile they asked him how he felt and he said, 'I'm in fine fettle.'
a few	a lot: *Ther wez a few theer. Aa hed tuh stan.*
flairt	frightened
flarch	verb = to flatter, wheedle; noun = a flatterer, sycophant
flaysome	frightening
flooer	(rhymes with sure) flower; flour; floor
fornenst	in front of
fratch	to squabble, argue
freh	from. (Pronounced like Scottish *frae* but with a shorter *eh* sound.)
f'yass	face
ga'an	going (past tense **went**):
	Ther yance wuz a feller fra' Dent
	As wanted to travel to Kent.
	When 'e got till the stayshin
	An axed Informayshin,
	They said 'Ther's nee train cos it's went.'
gadgee	a man, person. (a Romany word, especially used in Wigton)

galluses	braces. (Originally *gallowses* because your trousers hang on them.) 'Many a good hanging prevents a bad marriage' says Shakespeare in *Twelfth Night*.
gan	go
gansey	a pullover
gey	very: *T' myern's gey breet toneet.*
gezlin	a gosling, a young goose. (If you're too late to make an April fool of someone you can wait a month and make them a May gezlin.)
gitten	got: *Aa's gitten mesel a new gansey.* This ancient past tense crops up in other verbs. A traditional tale about one schoolboy sneaking to teacher about his neighbour's grammatical error ends, "He's been an putten 'putten' when he should've putten 'put'."
giz	contracted form of 'give us', meaning 'give me': *Gis a hand oot o this wholl.*
gomeral	an idiot
gowk	1. an apple core 2. a cuckoo 3. a fool. F.J. Carruthers (see BRAY) reckons there are at least 67 dialect words for calling someone a fool. (See also BORROWDALE p. 29)
gripe	a garden fork
grun	ground
g'yerss	a goose. (A comment on country gossip says of a piece of news, *If it's a fedder at Codbeck, it's a gyerss in Hesket.*)
haaf net	a huge, hand-held fishing net on a wooden frame, used to catch salmon in river estuaries. (The traditional pastime has lost its savour recently since the Inland Revenue have unsportingly taken to summonsing fishermen for not declaring the number of fish they catch.)
hesta?	have you? (hast thou?): the classic dialect phrase everybody quotes is *Hesta ivver sin a cuddy lowp a five-barred yat?* To which the reply is *Twas owther a lish cuddy else a laal yat.*
hev	have. Also **heh** or **ha'**, as in *T'rawds is gey slyape; thoo'll heh to ga canny.*

hevven't ter	mustn't: *Yuh hevven't ter gan in't field when't bull's theer.*
hod	to hold: *Hod thi pie* Wait a moment.
hog	a young sheep. Dry stone walls often have **hog holes** in them to let sheep move from one field to another. These can easily be sealed with a large stone or bit of hurdle.
hoo	how. See also WHEE.
i'	in: *Aa wuz i' church a Good Frida.*
ista?	are you? (ist thou?): *Oo ista?* How are you?
jam eater	a miner from Workington or Whitehaven. (It's either a derogatory term mocking the miners' poverty (jam was all they could afford) or refers to the fact that they couldn't take meat down the pit where the atmosphere would make it go off: *Wukinton's famous for coal an' steel; White'evven's famous for stealen coal.*)
jike	to tap or knock
Kersmas	Christmas
kessin	a fully-fleeced sheep fallen on its back can't get up. It is *kessin.* (If you see one stuck, tell the farmer or give it a helping hand.)
laal	little, small. Also lile; laal uns = children.
laik	to play
lait	to look for, search for:

> Yan o't shepherds, oot on't fell,
> When't angels come, good news ter tell,
> Paid nee heed til't Heavenly host
> But went to lait a yow e'd lost.

lish	agile
a lock	a lot: *Thers a lock o' fawk gans tuh Keswick for t' theatre.*
lonnin	lane: *'Theer it gans. Doon't red lonnin,'* says Mam encouragingly as the bairn swallows some awful medicine.
lowp	to jump
lug	ear: *If thoo doesn't give ower thoo'll git thi heed i' thi hands an thi lugs to play wid!*
lug marks	sheep used to be identified by specifically shaped slots clipped out of one or both ears

l'yerk	look
maizled	puzzled, bemused
maizlin	a stupid person
mak	sort: *It teks aw maks ter mek a wurld.*
mappen	perhaps
marrer	mate, friend. Borrowed from the Geordie miners who came to West Cumbria. It's often spelt *marra*, but this can be misleading. In 2006 a dolphin took up residence off Maryport and was christened Marra.
murry neet or **merry neet**	a celebration, usually involving music, tatie pot, and drink. These days it's generally a bit of a nostalgic evening celebrating the dialect.
mowdywarp or **mowdy**	a mole
mun	must: *Aa mun tek't weshin in afoor it rains.*
nash	to dash, run: *Nash it! 'Ere comes't farmer wid is dog.*
nee	no: *Aye, we hev nee bananas.*
nin	none: 'Have you any bananas?' *'Nee we've nin.'*
nobbut	only (a reduced form of *nowt but*)
nowt	nothing (nought): *T'was neether nowt nor summat.*

Oo ista?	How are you? Reduced to **oosta** in expressions such as *Oosta gaan on? Oosta d'yern?*
oot	out. See also OWT
ower	over (rhymes with power): *Aa was ower paggered ter climb ower t' waw an chess em.* I was too tired to climb over the wall and chase them.
owt	anything (aught)
owther	either
paggered	exhausted: *Aa's fair paggered.*
poddish	porridge; **poddish way roond** clockwise (as you stir your porridge)
poyetry	poetry
p'yapper	paper: *It mun be reet. Aa rid it int' p'yapper.*
ratch	to scrabble and search: *Aa wuz ratchin' aboot int' attic an aa fun me granfadder's awd gansey.*
reet	right; very, really: *They were reet maizled.*
recklin	the runt of a litter of pigs
scop	to throw
scran	food (Romany). Two Wigton lads in London decided to have some fun at the expense of a policeman. 'Scuse me, Marrer. Dusta knaw wheer't scran cower is?' asked one of them … 'Aye aa d'yer,' said the copper who had joined the Met from Cumbria Constabulary. 'An aa knaw thee, Billy Dobson. Aa yance arrested thi fadder fer drunk n' disorderly.'
scrant	hungry
sec	such: *sec a to-do on't beach* what a commotion on the beach
shaff	an expletive, *Oh shaff!*, rather stronger than Oh dear!
shut	to shoot (rhymes with soot)
sin	seen
sin'	since: *a weak sin'* is not a minor misdemeanour but 'seven days ago'; **lang sin'** long ago: *Me Granma deed lang sin.*
sista	a contracted form of *seest thou?*. It can mean look!: *Sista! A shuttin star*; or look at: *Sista yon lish lass*; or is just used to emphasise something, like the Welsh *Look you: That's nut his wife e's kissin. It's is sister, sista.*

skelp	to slap: *Is mam skelpt is backside.*
skinch	the word used to signal neutrality in children's games: *Thoo can't tig muh; aa's skinch*; the equivalent of expressions such as pax or fainites used in other parts of the country.
skit	to tease: Apprentice *T' gaffer's sent muh fer a lang weight.* Storeman *Well stop theer. An' divvent budge.* After ten minutes or so the apprentice realizes he has been skitted.
sk'yerl	school
sl'yap	slippery
sneck	a door latch: An unwelcome suitor who has the door slammed in his face is said to have *gitten a sneck possit.*
spatchcock	a cock killed and eaten at once; **to make a spatchcock of someone** was to inflict a particular type of punishment: the victim was left with his head stuck in a rabbit hole and his legs pegged to the ground!
spell or **spelk**	a small splinter: *Aa's gitten a spell i' me finger.* (The *g* in finger is pronounced as in 'winger' or 'singer'.)
stirk	a young bullock: I went to warn a neighbour her beasts were on the road. She wasn't surprised, *'They're nobbut laal bits o' stirky things.'*
stoor	dust: *Thoo wadn't see ther backs for stoor.*
summat	something
supper	the main evening meal
t' or **'t**	the (T' Lady in't Lake was the poor soul murdered and dumped in Coniston in 1976 and only discovered by divers 21 years later.)
tarn	a stretch of water bigger than a pond but smaller than a lake
thi	your (thy): *Eat up thi poddish.*
thoo	you (thou), sometimes shortened to **thuh**: *Aa'll give it thuh*; or **tuh**: *Whatt's tuh d'yern?*
thowt	thought: *thoo knaws whatt thowt did – wet hissel an' thowt 'e was sweatin'.*
thrang	busy: *Aa's ower thrang to laik aboot; Toon was that thrang aa hed to walk in't gutter.*

throssle	the thrush (Wigton claimed to be known as *The throssle nest of aw England* because of the quality of its singers.)
til t'	to the: *Gie's a ride up til t' byre*; to it: *T'yabble's laid. Gan til t'.*
trod	a footpath; a cattle track
tup	a male sheep
turrable	terrible but often used in the sense of awesome so that it becomes a kind of superlative: *Ah's turrable bad* I'm very ill; *John Peel wuz a turrable hunter* doesn't mean he was bad at it but that he was fanatically keen. A classic dialect story about a young girl sent to live in Dent describes the women of the town spending every minute at their needles: *They're turrable knitters i' Dent.*
twa or tweer	two
t'yabble	a table
t'yal	a tale
t'yan	taken: *Whee's t'yan me glass? Twassn't empty.*
t'yerth	a tooth
vanya	almost (a condensed form of *varra near*)
varra	very

Bus Stop Scene 2

A Local L'yerk at
Nursery Rhymes

The Grand Old Duke of York

wark	work (rhymes with bark). On November 5th an amazed lad said to his brother, 'Sista Billy, feerwarks.'
whatt	what (rhymes with mat) Rudyard Kipling wrote: 'I keep six honest serving-men/ They taught me all I knew. Their names are What and Why and When And How and Where and Who.' In Lakeland their names would be: *Whatt 'n' Whey 'n' When/ 'N' Hoo 'n' Wheer 'n' Whee.*
whee	who, when used as a question. In other expressions like 'the one who' it is replaced by *as: t'lass as wedded a gadgee fra Sp'yatry*; or *whatt: 'Im whatt won a gurnin' contest an' didn't knaw 'e'd entered.*
whisht	quiet, quietly: *Hod thi whisht!* Shut up!
wick	**1.** alive (quick): *the wick an the deed.* **2.** a maggot or tick (a living thing) on a sheep
wickt	(of a sheep) maggoty; no good, flawed A Cumbrian vicar met a shepherd: 'Good morning, Joseph. Tending your flock, I see. Just as I – ha ha – tend mine.' *'Aye, vicar. But if aa hed as many wickt uns i' mey flock as thoo hes i' thine, aa'd be oot of a job.'*
wid	with
widoot	without
wishin	a cushion
wholl	hole (rhymes with doll): *t'wholl in t' waw* – the cash dispenser
ya	See YAN
yaffle	the green woodpecker
yak	the oak
yam	home: *'Can aa set thuh yam?' 'Aw reet, but nee hanky panky!'*
yan or ya	one: *'Ivvery time aa hev a wesh aa use yan o' them bubble baths. Thoo should try it.' 'Mappen aa'll ev yan ya yeer.'*
yance	once
yat or yet	a gate
yow	a ewe
yubbin	an oven

THE LAKES

The first thing to remember – and certainly one of the things every local pedant will delight in telling you – is that there's only one *lake* in the Lake District. That's Bassenthwaite Lake, which is named after the village that stands by its shore. Every other large stretch of water is either a *mere* (Windermere, Buttermere, etc), or just a *water** (Ullswater, Crummock Water). Resist at all times the urge to call them Lake Thirlmere or Lake Wastwater. Don't even say Lake Bassenthwaite. Certainly Windermere lies next to a town of the same name, but the lake was there first. The town grew up round the railway station, which took its name from the lake.

Windermere is the longest, Wastwater is supposed to be the deepest, and Thirlmere is artificial. It was created as a reservoir for Manchester and when the valley was flooded the village of Mardale disappeared under the waters. You can see it occasionally in times of very dry weather.

*Or rather a *watter* in local usage. Keswick is flanked by *Darrenwatter* and *Bassenthet*, which is also known as The Bass Lake.

CHAPTER 3

Wheer are wuh?

Some local place-names

Aspatria   When locals are being formal it's pronounced as-pate-rea, but it's generally called sp'yatry. (It is NOT pronounced as-patt-ria.) The local porter on Aspatria station is said to have shouted 'Sp'yatry – lowp oot!', while his well-spoken but ignorant colleague was calling 'Asp-at-rear, change here!'

Borrowdale   Notable among other things as the wettest valley in England, it's also the Cumbrian equivalent of Ireland to the English or Poland to the Germans: the place where the daftest people live. This is partially based on the story of the *Borradle gowk* or Borrowdale cuckoo. Having heard the first one of the year, the locals built a wall across the mouth of the dale in order to imprison the cuckoo so that spring would never go away. As he saw it fly over the top, one of the builders moaned, 'By gow, if we'd nobbut laid ya mair course o st'yans, we'd uv hed im!' If you're in Borrowdale you could also visit the Bowder Stone.

Bothel   (pronounced bawl by some and boy-ll by others)
> 'Stragglin an' win'swep, on't edge of a knoll
> Is't canny laal Cummerlan village of Bothel'

wrote Willie Sanderson of Aspatria.

Brougham   (pronounced brewem – see Broughton) A village and castle near Penrith; the Romans called it *Brocavum*, which apparently means either the place of badgers or (my favourite) the pointy place. Nearby is a circular grass platform supposed to be King Arthur's round table. Has it occurred to you that, if the idea of the round table was for each knight to be equidistant from the king, Arthur must have sat on top in the middle, swivelling round continually to keep the conversation democratic? There's a horse-drawn carriage of the same name, presumably invented here.

Broughton   (pronounced braw-ton in polite circles, but otherwise brow-ton – see Burgh by Sands).

29

Burgh by Sands (pronounced bruff, like Brough on the A66) Burgh by Sands is where Edward I died on his way to hammer the Scots. I only mention this because the classic spoof book on English history *1066 and All That* jokes about the king dying at 'Burrow in the Sands', which used to puzzle me until I realized that the authors assumed the pronunciation was as the *burgh* in Edinburgh.

Caldbeck (locally pronounced codbeck). The beck isn't especially cold and certainly contains no cod. Caldbeck churchyard contains the graves of both Mary Robinson, The Maid of Buttermere and John Peel. John Woodcock Graves, who wrote 'D'ye ken John Peel', lived in the village. He said, 'I was cheated, robbed, and gulled to such an extent ... that I resolved to go to the farthest corner of the earth. I ... landed in Hobart Town, Tasmania in the year 1833'.

Carlisle (pronounced with the stress on the first syllable, not the second; locals pronounce it care'l) The name has nothing to do with an island. The Romans called it *Luguvallium*, which might mean the fort of Lugh, a Celtic god and, after the legions left, the natives translated this as Caerlwel. Carlisle is the only city in Cumbria and has what must be one of the most business-like castles in Britain. Its inhabitants are sometimes referred to as Castor-oilers.

Launching pad for Cumbria's entry into the Space Race.

Cockermouth Birthplace (almost simultaneously) of William Wordsworth and Fletcher Christian. It's at the mouth of the little river Cocker where it joins the big river Derwent.

> Ther yance lived a body i' Cockermooth
> As needed a padlock ter lock 'er mooth.
> She'd bledder an' blabber
> Till yuh wanted to stab er;
> Or pull back yer elbow an sock er mooth.

Cumdivock The 'cum' is Celtic, the same as Welsh *cwm* 'valley' and -divock is from an Old Welsh derivative of *du* meaning 'black', which may have been a personal name or a stream name. Robert Anderson, in one of his lyrics, points out that there are many related place-names:

> There's Cumwhitton, Cumwinton, Cumranten,
> Cumrangen, Cumrew and Cumcatch,
> And many mair 'Cums' i' the coonty;
> But none wid Cumdivock can match.

This is not because the village is particularly picturesque but because it contains the heroine of the ballad in question: sweet Sally Gray.

> For Sally, she's leyke allyblaster,
> Her cheeks are twee rosebuds in May –
> O lad ! Ah cud stan' here foriver,
> An talk aboot sweet Sally Gray.

Grasmere (sometimes pronounced gersmer) The famous Grasmere sports include fell racing, wrestling, and hound trailing. Athletic events include pole-vaulting, and it's said that one technique was to plant the pole upright and then climb up it to drop over the bar.

Haverthwaite (meaning 'oat clearing') Hands up anyone who didn't know a haversack was a bag to keep your oats in. There's a neat little railway at Haverthwaite, which takes you to Lakeside on Windermere.

Hesket Newmarket deserves recognition on two counts: firstly as the birthplace of Eddie Stobart – both the man and the haulage firm – and secondly because the village inn, the Crown, is probably the only pub in the country to be owned by its customers. When it looked as if the place might close down the villagers formed a co-operative and bought it. They also run the attached brewery.

Lamplugh (pronounced lampler) The place is remarkable for an uncanny number of unnatural deaths that occurred there between 1656 and 1663. Three old women were drowned as witches and other mysterious deaths included those of two beggars worried by a house dog, four stag hunters whose *cuddies* failed at a five-barred *yat*, one person led into a pond by a will-o'-the-wisp, and four who choked eating barley. Two more died in duels, the first of which was fought with frying pan and pitchforks, and the second with a jug and a three-foot stool.

Penrith Not to be pronounced with the stress on the second syllable as if it were somewhere in Wales or Cornwall; in dialect it's *peereth*.

Ravenstonedale It does actually mean 'the dale with the raven stone'. Nobody could ever be expected to give such a long word its full value, of course, and it is pronounced russendle. The church has a three-decker pulpit retained from the previous building, which also used to feature a so-called refuge bell. If an escaped prisoner could make it to the church and ring the bell, he was let off.

Sawrey (means 'a muddy place') The village is now world-famous as the home of Beatrix Potter; even the church is dedicated to St Peter.

St Bees The saint's name was actually Bega, and Melvyn Bragg's novel *Credo* tells you about him. The town is home to a famous public school which was founded by Archbishop Grindal and which even in the 1960s compelled its gangling, embarrassed sixth-formers to wear grey shorts! W. S. Gilbert (of 'and Sullivan') is supposed to have produced the first version of

> *There was an old man of St Bees*
> *Who was stung in the arm by a wasp.*
> *When they asked "Does it hurt?"*
> *He said "Not very much,*
> *It can do it again if it likes."*

Sebergham (pronounced sebberum) Most noteworthy for the seriously steep hills by which the road enters and leaves the village. From Penrith you swoop down Sebergham Brow into the village, do a couple of 90 degree turns over the beck and battle your way up Doctor's Brow to get out. HGVs regularly fail this obstacle course and stall halfway up Doctor's Brow, often rolling back and demolishing the grit-hopper which Cumbria County Council obstinately continues to site by the roadside.

Thornthwaite If you've been paying attention you've spotted that this means a 'clearing with thorns'. The landlord of the Swan Inn at Thornthwaite used to be responsible for painting the white stone on the steep fellside above the village. This marks the spot where a bishop came to grief after wagering that he could ride his horse over the mountain. The horse fell back and killed him. The Swan no longer exists; so I don't know who paints the stone now.

Torpenhow The famous Hill Hill Hill is actually pronounced truh-penner.

Urswick (pronounced uzzock) There's *Girt Uzzock* and *Laal Uzzock* and *Uzzock Tarn*, which is supposed to cover a sunken village. Two artists born in Urswick achieved national prominence: James Cranke (1707-81) and James Cranke (1746-1826).

Wasdale Will Ritson who farmed in Wasdale and ran the pub used to boast that *Wozdle* featured the highest mountain in England (Scafell Pike), the smallest church (St Olaf's), the deepest lake (Wastwater) and the biggest liar (himself).

Wreay (pronounced rear) Wreay is the site of a wonderful chapel, erected by a local resident, Sarah Losh, to her own design, which anticipated the Arts and Crafts movement, espoused by Coniston resident John Ruskin. It's a treasure-house of carvings and stained glass, and stuck in the walls are arrows in memory of Major Thain, who was killed by a poisoned arrow on the Khyber Pass. Wreay has its own parliament, the 'Twelve men of Wreay'.

Puzzle inscription from Caldbeck

CHAPTER 4

Lakeland Lads an' Lasses

Some notable Cumbrians

Melvyn Bragg

Lord Bragg of Wigton was born there in 1939 and still keeps a home in the county, though he spends most of his time in London supporting Arsenal (Shame!).

He is probably the most famous living Cumbrian, thanks to his novels, his television and radio programmes, his campaigning for the arts, and an accent that still retains a whiff of Cumbria. You can read all about his boyhood in his novel *The Soldier's Return* and its sequels. One of very few in those days to go on from the local grammar school to Oxford, he joined the BBC and spent some time working with the controversial film-maker Ken Russell. During this period he published the first of the novels set in his native county, which introduced a wide reading public to Cumbria and, often, the dialect*. *The Hired Man* has been turned into a successful stage show with music by Howard Goodall, and *A Time To Dance* got a fairly steamy TV adaptation. Neither in the West End nor on television did any actor really capture the accent, but the Theatre by the Lake in Keswick produced *The Hired Man* in 2005 and recruited local people for the chorus and small parts. The professionals still struggled but every now and then a line would ring out clear and true.

As head of arts at London Weekend Television Melvyn Bragg created *The South Bank Show* and pretty well single-handedly made the arts popular in all their forms from pop music to ballet, stand-up comedy to opera. His Radio Four discussion programme *In Our Time* is still one of the most entertaining items on radio, even when you haven't a clue what his guests are on about.

Lord Bragg has recently rung up what must surely be a first for a Cumbrian; his name has been adopted into Cockney rhyming slang and a *Melvyn* apparently is a 'shag'. A local paper modestly wondered whether this referred to a bird or a carpet.

The Oxford English Dictionary singles him out as the first writer to use the word 'prat' though this is not a dialect word.

Fletcher Christian

Born in 1764 at Cockermouth, the famous leader of the mutiny on the *Bounty* has probably been portrayed in the cinema more than any other Cumbrian – by at least two Americans and an Australian. Clark Gable played him noble and heroic in the face of Charles Laughton's sadistic Captain Bligh ('The man is dead, Sir. Shall I dismiss the men?' 'Certainly not! Fifty lashes!'); Marlon Brando brooded in an extraordinary accent; and Mel Gibson was frankly rather petulant.

The real Christian had been a protégé and friend of Bligh, and probably led the mutiny more out of his desire to get back to the dusky maidens of Tahiti than from humane outrage at his captain's harsh methods*. In fact many of the crew resented the lieutenant because Bligh seemed to give him special treatment. Once he was in command he did a good job of navigation in finding Pitcairn Island but the little colony he founded there soon fell apart. He died on Pitcairn in 1793, apparently killed by disgruntled Tahitians who had sailed with the mutineers and found them less superhuman than they imagined.

According to Bligh, Fletcher Christian was dark, bow-legged, and swore a lot. He was born into a wealthy family (they said Moorland Close, where he was born, had dog kennels better than most folks' houses) but ran away to sea at the age of 16 when his widowed mother went bankrupt. Her family are believed to have suffered from a rare genetic condition similar to Parkinson's disease and it may be that Fletcher Christian's greatest contribution to history was to take the disease out of Cockermouth and spread it round the world.

As the *Bounty* has been such a favourite of film-makers we should note that Midshipman Richard Young, one of the mutineers, was an ancestor of Errol Flynn.

Though it's a fact that Bligh later became Governor of New South Wales and there was a mutiny there too!

Brian Deacon

Brian was British Fashion Designer of the Year in 2007. He has designed women's clothes for Gucci and many other fashion houses. His is not a profession one would expect to associate with a lad from the Lakes, and the clothes he designs wouldn't last long on the top of Skiddaw, but he's a leader in his field and interviewers sigh about his 'dulcet Cumbrian tones'; so he deserves a mention in this book.

George Macdonald Fraser

Fraser was the son of a Scottish doctor in Carlisle and is probably best known as the author of the rollicking Flashman novels about the later life of the school bully from *Tom Brown's Schooldays*. Fraser's Harry Flashman is the ultimate Victorian cad; a complete coward and indefatigable ladies' man rogering his way through the Empire and every military campaign of the 19th century. He even manages to be the only survivor (apart from a horse) of Custer's last stand.

Fraser himself fought as a young man with the local Border Regiment in Burma. His memoir of those days, *Quartered Safe Out Here* is one of the best-ever studies of war at the very sharp end. His ear for dialect is spot on and the conversations he records between a section of Cumbrian infantrymen are as good a taste of the real thing as you'll get.

Other very funny books cover his time as an officer in the Gordon Highlanders and feature Pte McAuslan 'the dirtiest soldier in the world'. Plans to turn this into a TV series never quite materialized but Fraser has written some excellent screenplays, including the Dick Lester *Three Musketeers*. His book *The Steel Bonnets* is a major study of the Border reivers, who turned the Scottish borders into something like the Wild West during the 16th century.

He researches his novels thoroughly and is adept at putting Victorian non-PC prejudices into the mouth of his character Flashman. This might also be because he's a frank, outspoken and unrepentant reactionary himself; perhaps the funniest genuine curmudgeon around.

Edmund Grindal

Edmund Grindal of St Bees rose to be Archbishop of Canterbury during the reign of Elizabeth I, at which time another St Bees native, Edwyn Sandys, was Bishop of London. Grindal deserves mention because, true to his blunt Cumbrian roots, he defied Good Queen Bess and actually told her off. In Latin!

Elizabeth had taken against a practice of public preaching because the people who went to the very popular meetings sometimes got excited and caused a disturbance. (One thinks of Mrs Thatcher wanting to ban all football because of incidents of hooliganism.) Anyway Grindal and most of his bishops were reluctant to do away with an effective religious practice, and, when Elizabeth insisted, the Archbishop wrote her a long document suggesting that she was interfering in matters in which she had no jurisdiction. At the end he told her she was not qualified to pronounce on matters of faith and said 'Remember Madam, that you are a mortal creature' and warned her that she should adhere to God's will or expect a 'heaping up of wrath against the day of wrath'.

The Virgin Queen was not amused but she couldn't dismiss an archbishop, and she certainly couldn't cut his head off, however indignant she might be. Grindal was sequestered – put under house arrest at Lambeth Palace – and deprived of most of his powers. He lived for several years in isolation and frustration and died soon after founding the grammar school in his native town.

Irvine Hunt

A modern Lake poet and observer of local traditions and quirks, he was a close friend of Norman Nicholson and his serious verse is on a par, though there's less of it. He also published *Manlaff and Toewoman*, a collection of poems about a couple of cave people living in a post-nuclear world.

> This, said Manlaff proudly, is
> a wheel.
> Oh, good, said Toewoman.
> Well I've just invented it,
> said Manlaff.
> Splendid, said Toewoman, and
> what exactly does it do?
> Ah well, confessed Manlaff, I
> haven't quite decided yet.
> Toewoman frowned. If you had
> a lot of wheels, she said,
> we could build a house.
> No, no, said Manlaff, wheels
> are not for building with;
> wheels turn.
> Toewoman eyed the block of
> stone. If that's going to
> turn, she said carefully,
> wouldn't it be better if it
> weren't square?
> Ah, said Manlaff. Well, as a
> matter of fact, he said,
> I've decided not to call it
> a wheel after all.
> Just for now I'll call it
> a brick.

Stan Laurel

Eagerly claimed as a Cumbrian these days, although Ulverston, where he was born in 1890, used to be in the old county of Lancashire and he lived there only a very short time. Nevertheless, the only Laurel and Hardy museum in Europe is

Anudder reet clart thoo's got uz intil

in Ulverston and at least one visitor reports that the owner insists on re-enacting scenes from the films before he'll let you in.

Arthur Stanley Jefferson was the son of theatrical parents, and, when the family moved to Glasgow, he helped his father run the Metropole Theatre. In 1910 he went with the legendary Fred Karno troupe to America and understudied Charlie Chaplin for a time, although he was already a performer in his own right. He changed his name to Laurel because some superstitious prat pointed out that Stan Jefferson had thirteen letters in it – just as well perhaps: Jefferson and Hardy sounds more like a firm of gents' outfitters.

They met when they were both filming *The Lucky Dog* in 1919. Stan was the driving force of the team and wrote most of the material for their films. He resisted the siren call of his native Lakeland until 1947, when he and Ollie came over and made a speech from the balcony of Ulverston Coronation Hall.

Laurel and Hardy are still among the world's favourite comedians and The Sons of the Desert, their disciples ('fan club' is much too frivolous a term), honour their memory with zeal. Laurel was awarded an Oscar in 1961, sadly after Hardy was dead.

A beguiling urban myth claims that Stan was secretly the father of Clint Eastwood. Apparently an Italian newspaper published a photo of Clint in his spaghetti western period wearing a big soft grin and looking just like the moon-faced comedian.

Students of language will want to know that in other countries Laurel and Hardy become, amongst other things, Dick und Doof (Germany), Stan es Pan (Hungary), Holjjugi wah Ddungddungi (Korea) and Flip I Flap (Poland).

Norman Nicholson
Probably the most well-known Cumbrian poet after Wordsworth and the Lake School, he was invalided from the age of 16 by TB. He lived all his life in his native Millom, endlessly fascinated by the people, the town and the landscape around him. Examples of his work are in most anthologies of 20th-century poetry. His verse covers a wide literary range but many of the most striking pieces are inspired by his local affiliations.

Scafell Pike

Look
Along the well
Of the street,
Between the gasworks and the neat
Sparrow-stepped gable
Of the catholic chapel,
High
Above tilt and crook
Of the tumbledown
Roofs of the town –
Scafell Pike,
The tallest hill in England.

How *small* it seems,
So far away,
No more than a notch
On the plate-glass window of the sky!
Watch
A puff of kitchen smoke
Block out peak and pinnacle –
Rock-pie of volcanic lava
Half a mile thick
Scotched out
At the click of an eye.

Look again
In five hundred, a thousand or ten
Thousand years:
A ruin where
The chapel was; brown
Rubble and scrub and cinders where
The gasworks used to be;
No roofs, no town,
Maybe no men;
But yonder where a lather-rinse of cloud pours down
The spiked wall of the skyline, see,
Scafell Pike
Still there.

Only a local would get away with calling Scafell Pike a hill. Norman Nicholson is commemorated in his native Millom by a glorious stained-glass window in the church and by the Norman Nicholson Society, with members worldwide.

John Peel

Not to be confused with the late disc jockey, although his fame is based on a song. His mate John Woodcock Graves wrote *D'ye ken John Peel?* one evening when they'd been celebrating after a hunt. The tune has been adopted as, among other things, a regimental march of the Household Cavalry and of Cumbria's Border Regiment; which is now, sadly, incorporated into a conglomerate of

once-noble units under the collective title The Duke of Lancaster's Regiment. It is also the semi-official national anthem of Cumbria and at *murry neets* they even have competitions for singing it – unaccompanied.

Peel himself was a farmer from Caldbeck with enough income and spare time to indulge his sport of hunting practically every day, generally following it up by drinking. 'I never thought much of John Peel,' said Beatrix Potter when told that he once got so drunk he fell off his horse. She was probably ahead of her time in disapproving of hunting *per se*. In fact Lakeland hunts generally follow the hounds on foot and the sport is for working men rather than horsey types but the prejudice against blood sports still applies. John Peel's grave in Caldbeck churchyard (and quite a fancy thing it is too) was once desecrated by anti-hunt saboteurs.

The point locals will bore you with about the lyric of the song is that the first line refers to 'John Peel with his coat so *grey*', not 'gay': no hunting pink for Peel and his pals. They wore coats of hodden grey, woven from the wool of Herdwick sheep.

Beatrix Potter

Surely the only Lakeland resident to have her own 'world'. The World of Beatrix Potter attraction is in Bowness-on-Windermere and incorporates an exhibition of all the famous characters from her childrens' books: Peter Rabbit, Mrs Tiggy-Winkle, etc., plus an arts centre and theatre.

Beatrix was born a Londoner but said, 'Our descent – our interests and our joy – was in the north country'. She was educated at home and was rather shy, finding company in various pet frogs and newts and a rabbit called, as you've guessed, Peter. Her family used to come up to Cumbria for holidays and were friends of Canon Rawnsley*, the vigorous enthusiast for everything Cumbrian who almost single-handedly created the National Trust. When she died she left 15 farms, several cottages and 4,000 acres of land, first to her husband, and, on his death, to the Trust. Her farm at Hill Top, Sawrey is a shrine well worth a visit.

Beatrix is now also the subject of a film, *Miss Potter*, which concentrates on the love affair between the creatrix (?) of Mr Tod and Norman Warne, her publisher. He proposed by letter (while teaching her to dance in the film) in 1905 but died of leukaemia four weeks after they became engaged. The film has moments of poignancy but also of what Lady Bracknell called 'more than usually revolting sentimentality'.

*Canon Hardwicke Rawnsley also founded the Herdwick (pure coincidence) Sheep Breeders' Association, of which Beatrix became the first woman president.

When Warne died, Beatrix moved to The Lakes and settled in Hill Top. She took a huge interest in farming generally, buying other property, breeding sheep, judging at agricultural shows, and keeping an eagle eye on the doings of her managers and workers. 'Ah wish she'd git oot o't spot,' her sheepman Tom Storey used to say. In 1913 she married a local solicitor, Willie Heelis, whose own interest in animals and natural history seems to have been limited to keeping a ferret in his desk when he was a boy.

The charming books with their carefully-observed illustrations are popular throughout the world and have been translated into many languages. We can admire such melodious renderings as *Die Hasenfamilie Plumps*, German for the Flopsy Bunnies, whose names in France are *Flopsau*, *Mopsau*, *Queue de Coton*, and *Pierre*, and *Dili Minllyn*, the Welsh Jemima Puddle-Duck. If you're so minded you can even read *The Tale of Peter Rabbit* in Egyptian hieroglyphs! Beatrix Potter is enormously popular in Japan, where Peter Rabbit was one of the first English books to be published in translation and taught on the national curriculum. In Tokyo there's a chain of Peter Rabbit juice bars and a re-creation of Hill Top Farm in the children's zoo.

Mary Robinson

Known as The Beauty of Buttermere and celebrated in story, Victorian melodrama, and a novel by Melvyn Bragg, Mary was the daughter of the landlord of the Fish Inn at Buttermere and reputedly quite an adornment, though not such a beauty that her fame would have spread beyond Keswick in normal circumstances. Unfortunately, she was wooed, bewitched, and wedded by the last man to be hanged at Carlisle and so became a celebrity. The Lake Poets all popped round to have a look at her and wrote about her afterwards as a tragic figure.

The tragedy lay in the fact that the wooer, James Hatfield, was a fraud (pretending to be of noble birth when he wasn't), a forger, a sponger, and married already. When he was arrested in Keswick he made a fairly dramatic escape and was then hunted up and down the country, which brought the case to prominence. For a while afterwards Mary was definitely a tourist attraction and the Fish Inn did a roaring trade. She herself doesn't seem to have been too broken-hearted about everything and soon married a lad from Caldbeck, where she's buried.

Eddie Stobart

Generally pronounced *Stobbat* among Cumbrians. Strictly Eddie Stobart is the name of the famous haulage firm rather than of one man, since it was founded by Eddie Stobart senior of Hesket Newmarket but was turned into a national institution by his son Edward. Today it's run by another son, William, and a not quite so romantic bunch who are diversifying into rail haulage and even airports.

Eddie senior bought his first Guy lorry in 1960. 'Is he still interested in the Guy down at the garage?' they asked his wife over the phone. 'What's his name?' she replied.

Young Edward joined the business on leaving school and almost immediately began to push his own ideas for improvement. He took over the haulage side and moved base from Hesket to Carlisle. He took great pains to have clean lorries with the Eddie Stobart name prominently displayed, and gave each one a name. The first was called Twiggy: 'I rather fancied her at the time.'

He also pushed the philosophy of encouraging his drivers to take a pride in themselves and the firm by wearing smart uniforms, which originally included collar and tie. All this and the immaculate green, red and orange wagons got Eddie Stobart recognized up and down the country. Among other things, lots of people discovered you could sing the name to the tune of the Hallelujah chorus. The fan club was born!

Today club members can even nominate the names of loved ones to go on the wagons, though the waiting list at the time of writing was five years long. And there's merchandise. Look out for countless toy trucks, Eddie teddy bears, Eddie Stobart tattoos, even a lorry-shaped picture disc of 'I want to be an Eddie Stobart driver' recorded by The Worzels, which made the top 100 in 1995. Steady Eddie is a cartoon truck featuring in books and videos like a diesel-driven Thomas the Tank Engine. There's also *The Eddie Stobart Story* by Cumbrian writer Hunter Davies*, whose other subjects include The Beatles and Wayne Rooney. He'd be the first to remind you that when Carlisle won that cup at Wembley they were wearing green, red, and orange shirts sponsored by Eddie Stobart.

Apparently one of the attractions of Eddie Stobart is that people from outside this county simply find the name quaint and funny, something Cumbrians don't notice. If you want a real, gritty, local haulier's name, I recommend Tyson H. Burridge of Distington.

From which most of this material is gathered.

Alfred Wainwright

Through his meticulously drawn guide books and his homely, fluffy-eared wanderings on television, A. W. is arguably the man who brought the Lake District home to more people than anyone else. Conversely, since he also brought more people to the Lake District, he's the man most responsible for traffic jams in Wasdale and the erosion of the fell-tops. You can look at it either way.

Wainwright was born in Blackburn and remained a fanatical Blackburn Rovers supporter all his life – which, for my money, puts him on very shaky ground as far as his credentials as a Cumbrian are concerned – but he fell in love with the area early and lived most of his life in Kendal, working in the borough treasury and keeping drafts of his books in his desk drawer. We'll claim him as our own.

He was not a gregarious type and would even turn off the path and slip away if he saw bunches of ramblers coming his way. This shyness seems to have extended to his personal relationships and he would relate how his first wife 'went for a walk with the dog' one day and neither of them came back. Alone with his house and kitchen, he took to eating chips. He was luckier with his second marriage but really didn't go in much for companionship. He sometimes claimed he preferred animals to people and all the royalties from his books went into supporting Animal Rescue, Cumbria. He never saw the books as a commercial enterprise – he said, 'One does not wish to be paid for writing a love letter' – and his personal enthusiasm for the fells is at the heart of their appeal.

The celebrations for the centenary of his birth took place at Blackburn Rovers football ground.

William Wordsworth

Born in Cockermouth, he lived at Rydal and Grasmere with his sister and (a later addition) his wife, liked daffodils, and wrote poetry, including this description of a pond in *The Thorn*:

> I've measured it from side to side;
> 'Tis three feet long and two feet wide.

It's not difficult to mock some of his poetry (though the above couplet was removed from later editions), partly because he often wrote in a jaunty ti-tumti metre more suited to comic verse and chose superficially quaint subjects. The unfortunately titled *The Idiot Boy*, for instance, gives us

> Beneath the moon that shines so bright,
> Till she is tired, let Betty Foy
> With girth and stirrup *fiddle-faddle*;
> But wherefore set upon a saddle
> Him whom she loves, her Idiot Boy?
>
> ...
>
> And now that Johnny is just going,
> Though Betty's in a mighty flurry,
> She gently pats the pony's side
> On which her Idiot Boy must ride,
> And seems no longer in a hurry.

In fact the poem turns into a gripping story in which a seemingly inevitable tragedy turns to uplifting joy

Wordsworth was, of course, a great poet and should also be credited with creating the atmosphere which made the Lake District so popular and distinctive. His verses conjure vivid pictures of the landscape and people, and he wrote a *Guide to the Lakes*, which was famous in its own right. At least one person he met when he was Poet Laureate asked, 'Have you written anything else apart from the *Guide to the Lakes*?'

He got his income from being Distributor of Stamps for Westmorland, and his recreations included skating. He writes about it enthusiastically in the (very long!) poem *The Prelude* and was apparently so good he could cut his name in the ice. He was also fairly tight-fisted and failed to tip a boy who was sent to carry his skating gear. The lad got some satisfaction though: 'Did Mr Wudswuth give thee owt?' 'Nee. But Ah seed im tummle!'

The Yellow Earl

Hugh Lowther, the 5th Lord Lonsdale, was given this nickname because all his possessions, including cars, coaches, jockeys, and footmen, were decorated in his banana-coloured livery. The yellow survives on everything belonging to the Automobile Association, of which he was first president. He was fond of fast cars and you may remember that the AA was originally set up not as a breakdown service but to warn motorists of police speed traps*.

*Taking any action to warn drivers of speed traps was illegal; so the AA patrolman on his motorbike generally saluted every car he met which sported the AA badge. If he didn't salute, it meant there was a trap ahead.

Politically he stuck to his class and Cumbrian Tories still sport yellow rosettes instead of blue – to the consternation of the local Lib Dems. Something of a legend in his own lifetime, he crammed in a lot, including running away from home to join a circus, having an affair with an actress, and undertaking expeditions to the Arctic and to the USA, where he and some pals held up the Denver stage. This prank turned a bit sour when they found a postbag aboard and had to get away quick before they could be arrested for interfering with the US mail. As an American witness put it, they 'scattered like scared jackrabbits'. Which reminds us that he twice entertained the German Kaiser, who brought him a new Mercedes Benz. Wilhelm II enjoyed shooting rabbits (perhaps he was to see Belgium as just another bunny in 1914) so Lonsdale provided him with more sport than he may have bargained for. The Lowther gamekeepers collected every rabbit they could find and held them all in a wood to which the earl conducted his imperial visitor, remarking casually that they sometimes found the odd rabbit there. As the dogs went in the rabbits came out, pouring past the shooting party in scores, while the rattled Kaiser blazed away in all directions. Lowther was a fanatical sports enthusiast and is remembered in the supreme prize of British boxing, the Lonsdale Belt.

Lodore Falls in Summer

"How does the water come down at Lodore?"
A dry-season tourist once thought to explore,
But he failed to discover the famous cascade,
So enquired in despair of a Cumbrian maid,
"Indeed, Sir," quoth she with a toss of her bonnet,
"Ye may well seek Lodore, for ye're sitting upon it "

47

Some lesser-known people who crop up in Cumbrian conversation

Sister Yonda
Lyle Ladd
Tony Yann
Fred Earham
Hester Sinnim
Dee Caroon
Gay Wyatt
Mary Hurd
Les E Spock
Dean Accord
Lennie McCourt
Al Evitt
Our Gert
Russell Twiddit
Vanya Tummeltov
Evan Udder
Adam Orr

If you haven't quite spotted it the chat one winter night went:

Look at that little boy, the only one from Dearham. Have you seen him?
Look around.
Very quiet.
More he heard, less he spoke.
Dying of cold. Lend him a coat.
I'll have it. Too big. Wrestled with it. Nearly fell off.
Have another.
I had them all.

RED BANK, GRASMERE
(The steepest coach-road
in Lakeland)

Red Bank was steep, descent
   was rash,
Full soon there came a woe-
   ful smash.
A link snapped in the chain;
A passing native gave a
   shout
Of guileless satire "Eh,
   come out!
What! is ta flayt o' rain?"

CHAPTER 5

Games People Laik

Sports and pastimes

Cock fightin'

It's been illegal since 1835 but there were still illicit *mains*, as cockfights are called, in Cumbria well into the 20th century, and it may or may not still go on secretly. If it does, it's not confined to Lakeland, but the sport used to be very popular up here. In the 1970s a Mr Brownrigg stood for Parliament on a programme of home rule for Cumbria and re-legalized cock fighting. Breeders really pampered their birds, mixing arcane foods to build them up and foster a fighting spirit. The many breeds include Charcoal Blacks, Bonny Greys, and Black Reds, which is still the nickname of Aspatria rugby team, who battle gamely (a word taken from cock fighting) above their weight and have even matched professional sides like Wasps.

Hound trailin'

This is a sport for the dog-lover who wants to see foxhounds doing what they're bred to do best – run fast and tirelessly across country – without all the paraphernalia and dubious morality of a hunt. Very simply, a group of people bring their hounds to a meet, often at a village show or sports day, and stand holding them in until someone tramps onto the field pulling a sack filled with aniseed and other ingredients dear to a dog's heart and nose. An hour or so earlier, this person will have set off from nearby and walked through the countryside laying a circular trail for the hounds to follow in the reverse direction.

   As soon as they're released the dogs take off at speed and disappear into the wild, occasionally appearing on a fellside or through a gap in the trees. There's really nothing for spectators to do except pop into the beer tent for a pint and then stroll to the finish, where the owners have lined up with whistles, tins of food made to a secret formula, and other aids to bring their dog in first. As soon as the leaders appear everyone joins in an amazing cacophony of shouts, whistles, and banging of tins as they wave bright objects and one by one the dogs race home, some cocky and direct, some balking at a wall or fence, some going after a stray scent, and some apparently simply stupid, traversing back and forth across the field while their owner goes purple trying to attract their attention. It's good fun; the dogs really are glorious beasts, and there's betting. What more could you ask?

Fell running

Originally a straightforward race up and down a fell or two, if running up a gradient of one-in-two and leaping down rocks on the way back can be called straightforward. The early competitors werc professional mountain guides (at Grasmere Sports, for instance, the event is still officially the Guides' Race), who did it just for fun and a bit of money but now it's a sport for serious athletes. The greatest fell-runner of them all, Joss Naylor, competed mainly against himself, trying to see how fast he could cover literally every major peak in a day. His feats seem unbelievable to a layman, but he was bred on the fells and those who tend sheep up there do their daily round on heights which visitors, with their boots and anoraks, fibre walking poles and Kendal mint cake treat as a major expedition.

Gurnin' through a braffen

The big event, the World Championship, takes place each year at Egremont Crab Fair, which is a celebration of apples, not shellfish. A *braffen* is a horse collar and the skill of the contest lies simply in sticking your head through it and *gurnin'*, which is a dialect variant of *grinning*, but here means pulling the ugliest face you can. The results can be seriously disturbing and the starting point for many contestants is the ability to pull your lower lip over your nose! Not surprisingly success at gurnin' often runs in the family.

World's biggest liar contest

The idea is not simply to tell a lie but to spin the most imaginative and improbable yarn you can. The now world-famous event commemorates Will Ritson, a landlord of Wasdale who was notorious for his tall stories. It takes place at the Bridge Hotel in Santon Bridge and used to be a purely local affair involving mainly stories in dialect. The most successful participant until recently was undoubtedly John Graham of Silloth, whose outrageous, fantastic, and generally rather rude yarns won him the title five times. He still enters, but stubbornly (and rightly) ignores new rules and time limits that have been brought in as the event has become known through media reports and more entrants have appeared. In 2006 the inevitable happened and the world turned upside down when the chosen winner was non-Cumbrian, professional, and female: standup comedienne, Sue Perkins, who had only come along to record a Radio Four documentary and entered for fun. She had the good grace to be embarrassed about it and she herself thought that Graham was best, but you can't help feeling that a unique and thoroughly local tradition is in danger.

Cumberland and Westmorland wrestling

Russlin, as it's called locally, is said to have come in with the Vikings (of course!) but is unquestionably similar to Celtic wrestling, and Cumbrians often compete in international events in Brittany and elsewhere. The idea is simple: contestants grip each other round the neck and shoulders and try to throw opponents off their feet or break their hold. You mustn't undo your grip once you've started and the match begins with both wrestlers circling round feeling for the best purchase. When *B'yeth hod* ('both hold') is called by the referee, the struggle begins. It's not a flamboyant affair most of the time, a cross between ballroom

dancing for bears and slimline Sumo, but good bouts involve genuine skill and tactics, and winning throws can be pretty spectacular. Throws include the inside hype and the cross-buttock, and if both wrestlers fall together it's a dog fall.

Visual interest is added by the traditional dress of the wrestlers, which consists of old-fashioned white vests and long johns with velveteen pants worn on the outside, like Superman. These are often delicately embroidered, and a wrestling programme includes a prize for best-dressed entrant. Don't be fooled into thinking that the men inside the quaint outfits are in any way softies.

Uppies and downies

This no-rules ball game is played by the youth of Workington every Easter on a piece of land called The Cloffocks – which is probably as much as anyone needs to know. There are three matches, and rival teams (or mobs) compete to get a ball either up to Curwen Hall or down to the docks, using any means possible, which usually involves a massive scrum most of the time and players finding themselves in the river some of the time. No one has died for several years.

The winner is the one who can reach the target area and 'hail' the ball into the air in the presence of other players. This latter point is particularly important in matches like the first game of 2007, when an Uppie slipped the ball under his jacket, sidled quietly out of the melée and made his way, unnoticed, by back alleys to the hailing point. He had won but had to wait for an hour or so till the rest of the players noticed they were competing without a ball and, after casting about for a bit, finally found their way up to him.

CHAPTER 6

Cum to't Tyable

Local food and drink

> Ya word's as good as ten
> So wire in an' Amen.
> *(a Lakeland grace)*

Carlisle State Bitter

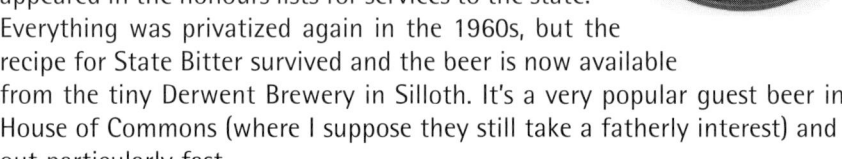

Carlisle brewery used to be remarkable as the only nationalized brewery in Britain. Together with all the local pubs, it was taken over by the Government during the First World War in order to control the drinking habits of munitions workers. The pubs became Government property, and landlords were civil servants who even appeared in the honours lists for services to the state. Everything was privatized again in the 1960s, but the recipe for State Bitter survived and the beer is now available from the tiny Derwent Brewery in Silloth. It's a very popular guest beer in the House of Commons (where I suppose they still take a fatherly interest) and sells out particularly fast.

Cumberland sausage

Spicy and meaty, this is proper sausage, in a thick rope, and you cut off as much as you think you need, which can be a foot or more per person. Each butcher has a private recipe, but the ingredients are pure pork and herbs, with nothing added for bulk. Cook it in the oven, coiled in a greased roasting tin. They even have it at Buckingham Palace.

Cumberland sauce

Nothing to do with Lakeland: it's a sauce named after Ernest, Duke of Cumberland, who was really a German, a brother of King George IV. He wasn't even that famous Duke of Cumberland popularly known as 'The Butcher' for the revolting things he did to the Scots after defeating Bonnie Prince Charlie. Still everybody thinks it's from up here and you'll certainly find it served in many of Lakeland's fine eating places. It's served cold to accompany meats and game pie.

Kendal Mint Cake

As taken by Hilary and Tensing on the 1953 Everest expedition, when a New Zealander and a Sherpa conquered the mountain for Britain. It comes in a flat cake like a bar of chocolate, but is made from more or less pure sugar; so it's a light, non-sickly source of energy, perfect for putting in a rucksack. The wrapper often boasts the many expeditions that have taken Mint Cake with them, to the point that one suspects more has been eaten in the Himalayas than in the Lake District.

The ingredients are sugar, glucose, and peppermint essence. It's white or brown, depending on the sugar and these days even comes covered in chocolate, though I don't think that really counts.

Tatie pot

Lakeland's traditional pot supper served at shepherds' meets, hunt suppers and *murry neets*. It ought to be made with Herdwick mutton (neck of lamb preferably) and black pudding layered in a casserole with potatoes and onions. Some people include carrots.

For four people take a pound of potatoes, a pound and a half of mutton, a black pudding and two onions. Slice everything and place alternating layers of potato, onion, meat and pudding; seasoning each layer and finishing with potato on top. Add half a pint of hot stock or water, cover the dish and cook for an hour and a half in a moderate oven (gas mark 4). Then brush the top with butter or dripping and brown in the oven for another half hour. Serve straight away with pickled red cabbage.

CHAPTER 7

Oor Mak o' Poyetry

Some dialect writers

There's a long tradition of verse-writing in dialect and some of it is even worth reading. Actually, the best is genuinely poetic and/or witty and would stand in its own right in any collection of good writing.

Robert Anderson of Carlisle was known as 'The Cumberland Bard' and had a prolific output capturing local events and characters. His ballads (they were written to be sung) tend to be a bit long, but, if you want a picture of country life and customs, they're a gold mine. Hard-living and ever ready to give to others he became almost penniless and disgruntled in later life. Somebody said that if you simply remarked 'It's a fine mornin' Mr Anderson' he would snap back, 'Dusta tek muh for a fyul? Ah kent that lang afoor aah met thee!'

John Richardson of St John's in the Vale. One of his characters is an old man:

> Ah's growin feckless, awld an I'yam;
> Me legs an arms are far freh't s'yam
> As whatt they used ter be.
> Me back oft warks an's seldom reet,
> Ah've scarce a t'yerth to chow me meat,
> An aah can hardly see.

The old chap sums up the culture of his youth:

> When aah was young folk used to larn
> To run and jump and russle, barn;
> T'was few that larnt to read.
> Folk thowt their lads was sharp an reet
> If they could use their hands an feet;
> T'was laal they cared for't heed.

But now he's out of his time:

> This warld an me are b'yeth alike,
> We're b'yeth ont shady side o't dyke,
> An tumbling fast doon't broo.
> There's nowt at aw that aah can see
> That's owt like whatt it used to be:
> Aw things is feckless noo.

Richardson's poem *Nobbut Mc* is popular enough to have been set to music by William Metcalfe, who composed the music to *John Peel*.

Edmund Casson of Keswick didn't write so much in dialect but he's worth including for this observation:

> I like to think of mountains thus;
> A wallowing hippopotamus.
> Helvellyn rolls its massy length
> In an uncouth and knotted strength,
> And the stray sleet-showers on its side
> Pick out the wrinkles in the hide.

A. C. Gibson of Westmorland could be earthy and grim telling of an old woman's terrible pet:

> Kyatey Curbison' cat hed of lives a lang lot;
> Yer may talk aboot nine, it hed ninety or mair.
> It was proof agyen puzzen, or pooder an shot;
> They had buried it yance but it still dudn't care.
>
> Kyatey Curbison' cat browt auld Kyatey to grief;
> Peer body, she nowder was comely nor rich,
> An't neighbours aboot settled doon to't belief
> 'At er cat was a devil an she was a witch.
>
> An they said, 'Let us swum er in't tarn,' an' they dud;
> She swom a laal bit an then drooned like a rat;
> An't cat aboot t'spot swom as lang as it could –
> An finished at last was Kyate Curbison' cat.

WHATT FETTLE, MUN!

William Sanderson of Sp'yatry worked for the local council and was a keen member of the Lakeland Dialect Society. His poem 'Aw Maks', about a local Quaker, could be set in any Lakeland town or village and will serve as a fitting send-off as you go on your further travels among us.

T'awld Whaker sat on't roadside seat,
Solemn an deep in thowt;
Musin' on't ways of man wid man
An't changes Time hed wrowt;
When up there cums a stranger chap,
Just newly cum til't toon;
A ootener, t'was plain to see,
Tekken a first l'yook roon'.

'Whatt sort o' fawks live here?' axed he,
An't Whaker meks reply
'Whatt sort, good friend, was them thoo left?'
Says't stranger, wid a sigh,
'Suspicious, narrer, mean as muck;
An maist unfair, Ah fear.'
'Ah's sorry, friend,' t'awld Whaker says,
'T'syam mak o' fawk live here.'

T' years rowled alang, until ya day,
It may soond radder queer,
Anudder stranger axed t'awld man,
'Whatt sort o' fawks live here?'
'Whatt kind were't neighbours thoo'd afoor?'
T'awld Whaker asks ag'yen:
'Finest in't world, a champion lot,
Good neighbours ivery yen.'

Beamed t'awld man's f'yass like't risen sun,
St'yull til his eye a tear;
'Then, friend, thoo'll fin,' was his reply,
'T'syam mak o' fawks live here.'

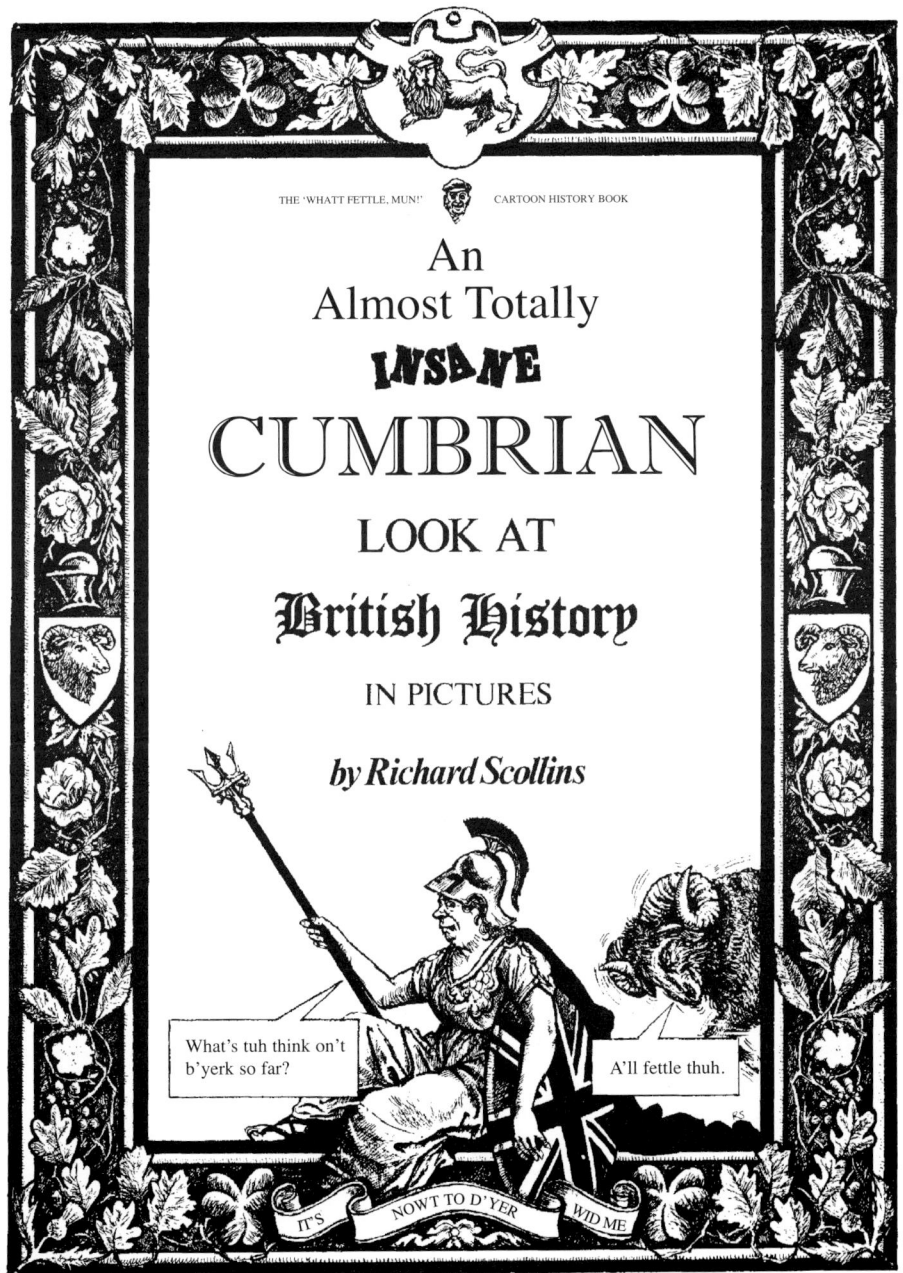

THE 'WHATT FETTLE, MUN!' CARTOON HISTORY BOOK

An
Almost Totally
INSANE
CUMBRIAN
LOOK AT
British History
IN PICTURES

by Richard Scollins

What's tuh think on't b'yerk so far?

A'll fettle thuh.

IT'S NOWT TO D'YER WID ME

Alfred and the Cakes – AD 878

Canute Demonstrates His Inability to Turn the Tide – AD 1020

Lady Godiva – AD 1057

The Battle of Hastings – AD 1066

The Death of William Rufus – 1100

King John and Magna Carta – 1215

Edward I Presents His Son as
Prince of Wales – 1284

Bruce and the Spider – 1306

The Battle of Agincourt – 1415

Richard III at Bosworth – 1485

Henry VIII and Anne Boleyn – 1529

Raleigh and the Puddle – 1581

Francis Drake Goes Bowling – 1588

The Execution of Charles I – 1649

**Charles II and Friends Hide From
the Roundheads – 1651**

Isaac Newton Discovers Gravity – 1666

**Bonnie Prince Charlie Arrives
in Scotland – 1745**

Wellington Inspects His Troops - 1815

The Charge of the Light Brigade – 1854

Stanley Greets Dr Livingstone - 1871

T'END.